Gay, Lesbian and Heterosexual Adoptive Families

Family relationships, child adjustment and adopters' experiences

Laura Mellish, Sarah Jennings, Fiona Tasker, Michael Lamb and Susan Golombok

Published by British Association for Adoption & Fostering
(BAAF)
Saffron House
6-10 Kirby Street
London EC1N 8TS
www.baaf.org.uk

Charity registration 275689 (England and Wales) and SC039337 (Scotland)

British Library Cataloguing in Publication Data. A catalogue record for this
book is available from the British Library

ISBN 978 1 907585 65 4

Designed by Helen Joubert Design
Printed in Great Britain by The Lavenham Press
Trade distribution by Turnaround Publisher Services, Unit 3, Olympia
Trading Estate, Coburg Road, London N22 6TZ

BAAF is the leading UK-wide membership organisation for all those
concerned with adoption, fostering and child care issues.

Contents

Acknowledgements

We would like to thank the Economic and Social Research Council for funding the research, and the British Association for Adoption and Fostering for their guidance and support. We would also like to thank all the local authorities, voluntary adoption agencies and parenting organisations, in particular New Family Social, for help in recruiting the participants for the study. The biggest thank you goes to the families who participated in the research; it would not have been possible without them! Thanks are also due to Professor Sir Michael Rutter for his insightful comments and Dr Caroline Fell for conducting the children's psychiatric ratings.

Authors

Laura Mellish graduated from Sheffield Hallam University in 2010 with a Bsc Hons degree in Psychology. She has worked as a researcher at the Centre for Family Research on projects examining different family structures, including families created through assisted reproduction and most recently same-sex and heterosexual families created through adoption.

Sarah Jennings completed her undergraduate degree in Social and Political Sciences at the University of Cambridge in June 2009. She worked as a Research Assistant at the Centre for Family Research investigating gay and lesbian family life with a particular focus upon qualitative data analysis.

Fiona Tasker, PhD, is a Senior Lecturer in Psychology at the Department of Psychological Sciences, Birkbeck University of London. She has specialised in family psychology and systemic family therapy. Her particular research interests have focused on gay, lesbian, bisexual and transgender parenting and GLBTQ affirmative systemic family therapy. She is the Editor of the *Journal of GLBT Family Studies*.

Michael E. Lamb is Professor of Psychology at the University of Cambridge. He has a PhD in Psychology from Yale University (1976), honorary doctorates from the Universities of Goteborg (1995) and East Anglia (2006), and received the James McKeen Cattell Award from the Association for Psychological Science for Lifetime Contributions to Applied Psychological Research in 2003/04. He has authored or edited about 45 books, including *Infant–Mother Attachment*, *The Role of the Father in Child Development*, *Child Care in Context*, *Child Sexual Abuse: Disclosure, delay and denial*, and *Children's Testimony*.

Susan Golombok is Professor of Family Research and Director of the Centre for Family Research at the University of Cambridge. Her research examines the impact of new family forms on parenting and child development. She has pioneered research on lesbian mother families, gay father families, single mothers by choice and families created by assisted reproductive technologies including in vitro fertilisation (IVF), donor insemination, egg donation and surrogacy. In addition to academic papers she is the author of *Parenting: What really counts?* and co-author of *Bottling it Up, Gender Development*, and *Growing up in a Lesbian Family*.

Foreword

In February 2013, two Bills appeared before Parliament – the Marriage (Same Sex Couples) Bill and the Children and Families Bill. The first marked another (controversial) step in establishing an equitable, fair and just society. The second is equally controversial in that it proposes the deletion of the current clause that requires adoption agencies to give due consideration to a child's racial origin, culture, religion and language. If the first Bill marks a step in giving due recognition to diversity, the second moves determinedly in the opposite direction, even if its intention is to improve the likelihood of a child from a minority group being placed for adoption. It is an odd combination of progress on the one hand, and confusion about the nature and position of minority identities on the other.

There is nothing new in this. When the current adoption legislation, the Adoption and Children Act 2002 (England and Wales), was debated in Parliament, there was considerable opposition and controversy because for the first time it proposed to allow same-sex couples to adopt jointly. The Bill was complex and detailed with a number of human rights issues, given the enormity of severing a child's legal relationship with their birth family, but the issue of gay and lesbian adoption was one of the issues that caught the heated attention of Parliamentarians. The clause that allowed same-sex couples to adopt did pass into law and was enacted in 2005, and the Cambridge study is the first to evaluate the impact of that change. In fact, it is the first in the UK to evaluate the outcomes for children of being adopted by gay fathers and to compare these outcomes to lesbian and heterosexual couples. The methods used by the Cambridge team, the robust data collected by them and the personal narratives from the interviews are compelling. Here we have a comprehensive and positive picture of adoptive family life marked by a child-centred, determined, resilient and sensitive set of values embedded in the reality of everyday life. And that is not to underestimate the challenge of negotiating the complex processes of becoming approved as gay adopters, establishing an adoptive family life, or facing the uncertainty of what is to come.

The Cambridge study is a good news story. Research generally indicates that in terms of developmental recovery from a poor start in life, adopted children do very well across a range of important dimensions. As a powerful intervention in the lives of vulnerable children, that is an important message. However, that is far from a straightforward message. There are enduring effects from early exposure to a variety of environmental factors and that includes, from some studies, prolonged institutional care. In the UK context, early institutional care is not so relevant but maltreatment, exposure to legal and illegal substances and other stressors pre-birth and a high loading of genetic risk factors most certainly are. Children adopted from care are likely to need a prolonged period of adjustment to a loving, ordinary adoptive family life and we know that for some this is a real challenge, whatever the social status of the adopters.

These are well known issues and this study is highly important and makes a major contribution for two reasons. The first connects to the issues raised above about legislative and societal change. The overall positive messages about outcomes from the study, especially when there has been significant doubt or opposition to making such placements, should reassure and positively support further developments in placing children with gay and lesbian couples. At a time when there are many children with adoption as the plan but a shortage of suitable adopters, the message to the gay and lesbian community must be inclusive in identifying them alongside other prospective adopters, whatever their social status. But that should not blind us to the potential and the reality of family lives that are marked by dimensions of difference. While the general direction of travel is to normalise such differences, not just in relation to sexuality but racial origin, culture, religion and language as well, there are many who believe that this should not happen. And the debate and vote in the Commons on the Marriage (Same Sex Couples) Bill powerfully evidences that. Difference is a feature of adoptive family life and it impacts on the child and the adoptive carers in many ways as they construct their lives together. Difference needs to be a part of the narrative of adoptive family practice where it is experienced and encountered, both inside and outside of the family. It may enrich, it may distress but its presence can be assumed. The study powerfully evidences this throughout.

The Cambridge study is to be savoured, digested and reflected on. It is a powerful, unique study. It is a good news story but it does not ignore the challenge. It reflects the best of adoption and it accepts the challenge. What more can one ask of a modern research study?

John Simmonds
Director of Policy, Research and Development, BAAF

Introduction

Since the introduction of the Adoption and Children Act 2002 and the Civil Partnership Act 2005, many lesbian and gay couples have started families through adoption; yet, to date, research on same-sex parent families has almost exclusively focused on families in which children were conceived through a heterosexual relationship or assisted reproduction. What is more, despite a large body of evidence regarding lesbian mother families, there have been few studies of children's adjustment when raised by gay fathers. The circumstances of gay father families are more unusual than lesbian mother families; not only are the parents same-sex, but it is also rare for fathers, be they heterosexual or gay, to be the primary caregivers. It is not known what the combined effect of these two factors might be on children's social, emotional, identity and gender development as they grow older.

This study was the first to examine families in which children live, from early childhood, with their adoptive gay fathers, lesbian mothers or heterosexual parents in the UK. The focus was on the quality of parent–child relationships, parental well-being and child psychological development. Our aim was to produce robust evidence that may be used to inform all those who work with lesbian and gay adopters and their children about the experiences of adoption and family functioning in same-sex parent families.

Names and identifying information have been changed.

On the following pages, we present a report highlighting the key findings.

1 What did we do?

This project explored family relationships, parental well-being and child adjustment in three kinds of adoptive families: those headed by gay fathers, lesbian mothers and by heterosexual parents, all of whom were couples.

One-hundred-and-thirty families (41 gay fathers, 40 lesbian mothers and 49 heterosexual parents) were primarily recruited through local authorities and voluntary adoption agencies, while some same-sex couples were recruited through gay and lesbian parenting groups. Children were aged four to eight years, with the exception of two children who were approaching four years old and two children who had just passed their ninth birthday. All children had been placed with their families for at least 12 months.

The final sample was recruited through 71 local authorities and adoption agencies; all involved English, Welsh and Scottish based adoptions from care.

Due to the large number of adoption agencies involved in the recruitment procedure, it was not possible to calculate accurate response rates. However, for those that kept systematic records, a participation rate of 71 per cent for same-sex parents was obtained. Currently there are no comprehensive data available on the gay and lesbian population; thus working out the representativeness of the sample is problematic. However, national statistics show that approximately 60 children are adopted by gay couples and 60 by lesbian couples in the United Kingdom each year (Department for Education, 2010). Given that these figures apply to children of all ages, our sample of 41 gay and 40 lesbian families with children aged four to eight years appear broadly representative of the currently small population of same-sex adopters.

Families were visited at home by a trained researcher who administered a range of measures:

- An interview was conducted with both parents, which focused on family relationships, parents'

adoption experience, including their route to parenthood, and child development and behaviour.

- Information on the psychological risk factors often experienced by adopted children was also obtained, such as length of time in care and number of pre-adoptive placements.

- Both parents completed questionnaires that assessed child behaviour, parenting stress, couple relationship satisfaction, social support and mental health.

- Two observational tasks were conducted with each parent and child, investigating parent–child interaction.

- A questionnaire was sent to the child's teacher regarding the child's behaviour at school.

- A short interview, conducted with the child (if he or she were old enough and willing to talk to the researcher), included questions on family, friends and school.

Parents were labelled as Parent A or Parent B. Parent A was assigned to the primary caregiver, and in heterosexual families Parent A was the mother. Parent B usually spent more time in employment and slightly less time with the child; in heterosexual families, Parent B was the father. In cases where parents shared their childcare responsibilities evenly, Parent A and Parent B were assigned randomly.

Reports of the research findings refer to "no differences", or a difference of "significance". These terms refer to the statistical analyses carried out on the data. Thus, "statistical significance" means that in only five per cent of cases was this finding likely to have been by chance. In contrast, when "no difference" is referred to, it indicates that, even when small differences may be noticeable between the three family types, they weren't large enough to be of statistical significance.

2 Parent characteristics

Data were gathered on the demographic characteristics of the three family types to examine similarities and differences between them. Findings were as follows:

- Parent A was of a very similar average age (40–43 years) across all family types. Ages of all Parent As ranged from 26–62 years old.

- There was a significant difference in the age of Parent B between family types, with gay fathers being younger than heterosexual fathers and lesbian mothers. Ages of all Parent Bs ranged from 28–62 years old.

- The parents were predominantly white.

- The socioeconomic status of parents did not differ between family types, with the majority in a professional or managerial occupation.

- Parent A came from a similar educational background in all family types, with a similar percentage in each group having acquired a degree or higher qualification.

- A significant difference was found between family types in the educational background of Parent B, with heterosexual fathers less likely than same-sex parents to have a degree or higher qualification.

- Heterosexual parents were significantly more likely to be married than lesbian mothers and gay fathers.

- All parents had been in their current relationship for a substantial amount of time, with a range of 5–30 years.

Figure 1: Parent characteristics

	Gay fathers	Lesbian mothers	Heterosexual parents
Parent A ethnicity:			
White	95%	87.5%	100%
Parent B ethnicity:			
White	93%	95%	92%
Socioeconomic status:			
Professional/managerial	90%	82.5%	73%
Skilled manual/non-manual	10%	17.5%	27%
Parent A education:			
Degree or higher	56%	68%	63%
Parent B education:			
Degree or higher	78%	82%	55%
Marital/civil partnership status:			
Married/civil partnership	73%	77.5%	94%
Duration of cohabitation (years)	12	12	16

3 Parents' well-being

Parents' well-being was assessed on a range of indices, using questionnaires; indices included measures of depression and anxiety, parenting stress and relationship problems.

A score above a certain point on each of these scales suggested that parents may have been suffering from depression, anxiety, parenting stress or relationship difficulties. The proportion of parents who fell into those categories are shown below.

A significant difference was found between family types for depression, with heterosexual mothers being more likely to experience depressive symptoms compared to gay fathers; heterosexual mothers did not differ from lesbian mothers.

Although it can be seen that heterosexual mothers, overall, tend to be more likely to experience problems than gay fathers, this study found no significant differences between family types other than for depression for Parent A.

Parent A

Depression
- 7% of gay fathers suffered from possible depression.
- 17% of lesbian mothers suffered from possible depression.
- 25% of heterosexual mothers suffered from possible depression.

Anxiety
- 10% of gay fathers suffered from possible anxiety.
- 17% of lesbian mothers suffered from possible anxiety.
- 18% of heterosexual mothers suffered from possible anxiety.

Parenting stress
- 10% of gay fathers experienced high parental stress.
- 16% of lesbian mothers experienced high parental stress.
- 24% of heterosexual mothers experienced high parental stress.

Relationship problems
- 3% of gay fathers experienced relationship problems with their partner.
- 8% of lesbian mothers experienced relationship problems with their partner.
- 13% of heterosexual mothers experienced relationship problems with their partner.

Parent B

Depression
- 3% of gay fathers suffered from possible depression.
- 15% of lesbian mothers suffered from possible depression.
- 19% of heterosexual fathers suffered from possible depression.

Anxiety
- 0% of gay fathers suffered from possible anxiety.
- 8% of lesbian mothers suffered from possible anxiety.
- 11% of heterosexual fathers suffered from possible anxiety.

Parenting stress
- 3% of gay fathers experienced high parental stress.
- 16% of lesbian mothers experienced high parental stress.
- 18% of heterosexual fathers experienced high parental stress.

Relationship problems
- 3% of gay fathers experienced relationship problems with their partner.
- 6% of lesbian mothers experienced relationship problems with their partner.
- 12% of heterosexual fathers experienced relationship problems with their partner.

Gay fathers were significantly less likely to experience stress associated with parenting, compared to both lesbian mothers and heterosexual fathers.

Again, it can be seen that heterosexual fathers have slightly more problems, overall, than gay fathers. However, this study found no significant differences between family types for Parent B on depression, anxiety or relationship problems.

Compared to mental health statistics published by the Mental Health Foundation, which estimates that 25 per cent of the general population will experience some kind of mental health problem, this sample does not have raised levels of problems. It is also important to note that the questionnaires completed by parents were not diagnostic assessment tools; they simply suggested the presence of possible psychological problems.

Parents were also asked to complete a questionnaire indicating how much support they received from their partner, family and friends. A significant difference between family types was found for Parent Bs, with heterosexual fathers perceiving less social support from their partner and friends than lesbian mothers did. There were no significant differences in the levels of support that Parent As felt they received.

Overall, both Parents A and Parents B in all family types had similar low levels of psychological and relationship problems, although there was a slightly higher tendency for heterosexual parents to experience problems than same-sex parents. However, compared with the general population, the parents were functioning well.

4 Children's characteristics

Data were collected on the children's demographic characteristics in the three family types to examine similarities and differences between them. The findings were as follows:

- Children had a similar average age of 72–76 months (6 years). Ages of all children ranged from 47–110 months old.
- Significantly more boys had been placed with gay fathers than with heterosexual parents and lesbian mothers.
- The majority of children had at least one sibling, either adopted or otherwise.
- Gay fathers had adopted older children than had heterosexual parents.
- Gay fathers' children, at the time of the study, had been placed with them for shorter periods of time than heterosexual parents' children.
- Gay fathers had also adopted children who had been in care for longer than those adopted by heterosexual parents.
- All children had had a similar number of pre-adoptive placements, with an average of two placements.
- Children in all three family types had experienced similar levels of abuse, pre-adoption.

Overall, the children were of a similar background and had comparable characteristics. Where differences were identified, they were found between the children of gay fathers and those of heterosexual parents.

Figure 2: Children's characteristics

	Gay fathers	Lesbian mothers	Heterosexual parents
Sex of child:			
Male	78%	40%	51%
Female	22%	60%	49%
Number of siblings:			
None	29%	32%	20%
One or more	71%	68%	80%
Care experience and placement details:			
Age child taken into care (average months)	17	15	10
Length of time in care (average months)	23	19	17
Child age at placement (average months)	40	36	27
Child length of placement (average months)	33	40	45
Number of pre-adoptive placements	1.66	1.73	1.55
Proportion of children who suffered abuse pre-adoption:			
Neglect	78%	63%	59%
Physical abuse	15%	20%	14%
Sexual abuse	2%	3%	4%
Emotional abuse	46%	45%	31%

5 Children's well-being

Children's well-being was measured in three ways:

- Psychiatric ratings – completed by a child psychiatrist.
- Strengths and Difficulties Questionnaire (SDQ) – completed by Parent A.
- Strengths and Difficulties Questionnaire (SDQ) – completed by the child's teacher.

Psychiatric ratings

Parent A was interviewed about their child's behaviour and development. Details of any emotional or behavioural problems were transcribed and sent to a child psychiatrist, who provided a rating of severity and type of disorder, if any. The psychiatrist was unaware of the child's family type.

Type of disorder was rated as emotional, attachment, developmental, conduct or hyperkinetic. Severity was rated as slight or marked. The results of these ratings are captured below.

Thirty-five children (27%) in the sample were classified as having a psychiatric disorder (20 with a slight disorder and 15 with a marked disorder).

Figure 3 shows that a slightly lower percentage of children with lesbian mothers (20%) and gay fathers (24.4%) had a disorder compared to those of heterosexual parents (34.7%). However, there was no significant difference between family types; thus the proportion of children with a psychiatric disorder was similar in all three family types.

Of the children classified as having a psychiatric disorder, five had an emotional disorder, 11 had an attachment disorder, 18 had a developmental disorder, and one had hyperkinetic disorder. Figure 4 shows the percentage of children in each family type with these disorders. There were no significant differences between family types in the proportion of children classified as having each of these disorders.

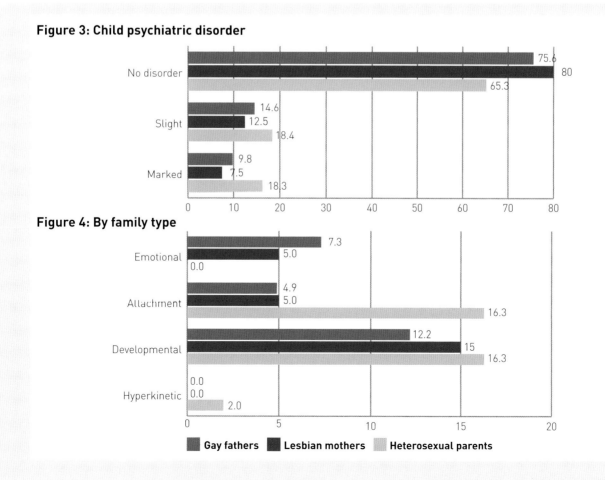

Figure 3: Child psychiatric disorder

Figure 4: By family type

■ Gay fathers ■ Lesbian mothers ▪ Heterosexual parents

Parent and teacher SDQ

Children's psychological problems were also assessed using the Strengths and Difficulties Questionnaire (SDQ), which assesses the presence of psychological problems. Parent As completed this to obtain a measure of the children's behaviour at home; children's teachers also completed the SDQ to gain a measure of the children's behaviour at school.

One-hundred-and-one teachers completed the SDQ, with an even distribution between family types (32 gay fathers, 30 lesbian mothers and 39 heterosexual parents).

The SDQ comprises five subscales: conduct problems, hyperactivity, emotional problems, peer problems and prosocial behaviour. A score above a certain point on a subscale suggests that a child has a problem beyond the range considered normal. Reported below (see Figure 5) are the proportions of children in each family type who fell into this category for each subscale.

Parent SDQ

A significant difference between family types was found on the hyperactivity subscale, with children of heterosexual parents rated as more hyperactive than children of gay fathers and lesbian mothers. No other differences were found between family types.

Teacher SDQ

No significant differences between family types were found for any of the subscales.

We also assessed children's gender role behaviour by asking parents to fill out the Pre-School Activities Inventory, a measure of children's masculine and feminine behaviour. No differences were found between children in the different family types, for either boys or girls. This is of interest, as the question of whether having same-sex parents affects children's gender-role behaviour is often raised; there was no evidence to support this speculation.

> From these results, it appears that children with same-sex adoptive parents are no more likely to suffer from psychological disorders than children with heterosexual adoptive parents. Neither do they differ in gender role behaviour.

Figure 5: Parent and teacher SDQ

Gay fathers:	Parent SDQ	Teacher SDQ
Conduct problems	22%	16%
Hyperactivity	20%	25%
Emotional problems	10%	0%
Peer problems	10%	13%
Low prosocial behaviour	2%	22%
Lesbian mothers:	Parent SDQ	Teacher SDQ
Conduct problems	28%	10%
Hyperactivity	18%	23%
Emotional problems	13%	7%
Peer problems	23%	3%
Low prosocial behaviour	5%	7%
Heterosexual parents:	Parent SDQ	Teacher SDQ
Conduct problems	25%	21%
Hyperactivity	35%	41%
Emotional problems	8%	10%
Peer problems	16%	8%
Low prosocial behaviour	4%	13%

6 Children's adjustment

A section of the interview with parents focused on children's experiences at school and with their peers.

The vast majority of children (93–97%) either mostly or completely enjoyed going to school. There was no difference between family types in relation to these questions.

Children were asked what they particularly liked about school and reported very typical things:

> **Toby, 5, child of lesbian mothers:**
> *'I get to play with friends in the playground and I get to do maths.'*

> **Keira, 5, child of gay fathers:**
> *'When it's been raining we go inside and do some games and that's my favourite.'*

> **Alice, 6, child of heterosexual parents:**
> *'They let us go outside, we also play and I actually really like playing.'*

> **Rachel, 6, child of gay fathers:**
> *'I like going on the computers at school and reading, at the moment I'm reading two chapter books.'*

> **Rory, 7, child of heterosexual parents:**
> *'Well, because you get to have five play times!'*

> **Laila, 7, child of gay fathers:**
> *'The teachers are friendly.'*

Parents were asked about any problems their children were experiencing at school in terms of misbehaviour; 54 per cent of heterosexual parents' children, 78 per cent of gay fathers' children and 65 per cent of lesbian mothers' children showed no problem behaviour at school. However, children of heterosexual parents misbehaved slightly more seriously and slightly more often than children with gay fathers.

In terms of adjustment with peers, there were no differences between family types, with three-quarters of children in each family type having no reported incidents of aggression towards peers.

In terms of making friends, we found no differences between family types, with all children having a similar number of friends and finding it equally easy or difficult to make friends. In general, the majority of children did not have problems making or keeping friends, and were not being picked on; 90 per cent of gay fathers' children, 80 per cent of lesbian mothers' children and 80 per cent of heterosexual parents' children were rated as having no problems or trivial problems with their peers.

Children were also asked about their peer relationships and, in each family type, 33 per cent of children reported being bullied or teased, and 92 per cent of these were teased for trivial reasons.

> **Sam, 6, child of lesbian mothers:**
> *'He sometimes, when he's in a bad mood, tries to kick me.'*

Only two children reported being teased because they were adopted, with comments suggesting that they weren't as lucky as children who were with their biological parents. Homophobic bullying, specific to children with same-sex parents, is discussed later in the report.

Most children had friends outside school. However, children of gay fathers were more likely to have active friendships and reportedly saw their friends more often than children with lesbian mothers and heterosexual parents.

Overall, the majority of children in all three family types were adjusting well to school, as indexed by enjoyment, behaviour and friendships. Children of same-sex parents were not experiencing greater problems at school and in peer relationships than those with heterosexual parents.

7 Parent–child relationships

Detailed information was gathered from parents about their family lives and relationships with their child. The results were organised into three areas:

- *Warmth/sensitivity*: parental warmth, relating to affection and sensitivity to the child's needs.
- *Interaction*: parents' enjoyment of play, amount of time spent with the child and the quality of this time.
- *Conflict*: level and frequency of parents' battles with the child and aggressiveness or indulgence when disciplining the child.

For Parent A, a significant difference was found with respect to *interaction*, with gay fathers having interactions of more positive quality than both heterosexual and lesbian mothers. No differences were found for *warmth/sensitivity* or *interaction* between family types.

For Parent B, a significant difference was found with respect to *conflict*, reflecting higher levels of disciplinary aggression by heterosexual fathers compared to gay fathers. No differences were found between family types for *warmth/sensitivity* or *interaction*.

We also used an observational measure to look at the way in which parents interacted with their child, so as not to rely solely on parents' reports of their own behaviour. The measure involved a short play task in which the child and parent were asked to work together. Parent A and their child were asked to draw a picture of a house together on an Etch A Sketch toy. Parent B and their child were asked to build something together with a set of building blocks. Video recordings were coded for signs of positive and negative interaction, such as tone of voice, praise, criticism and responsiveness.

There were no differences, in general, for either parent between family types; there was very little negativity or conflict and there were high levels of positive parent and child behaviour.

Information was obtained from parents about their view of their relationship with their child; for example, whether they found it easy to be affectionate with each other, the nature and extent of conflict and the development of the parent–child relationship.

The majority of parents were very positive about their relationships with their children.

'I feel really in connection with him and he's an easy child to sort of bond with and he's very loving and caring and he's very easy to love, to me.'
(Gay father)

'I think we get on great, I think we've got a lovely relationship, I like that – I suppose not neediness but sort of – I like the fact that he wants me there when he's doing things, he wants to show me things if he's achieved something. I think it's lovely he wants to spend time with us, he wants us to be there, he doesn't want to play by himself he wants to play with us, I think it's a lovely relationship.'
(Lesbian mother)

'We get along very well, we have a very loving relationship, lots of cuddles, she tells me she loves me a lot, I tell her I love her. We have a routine, I tend to be the one who reads her a story at bedtime ... we have a bedtime routine as well of magic cloaks and magic wands and it used to be a way of her ... if she was feeling sad or insecure or anything ... we'd tell her that magic cloaks were made of love and they keep her protected from bad dreams and stuff, and the wands seal the deal but now it just tends to be more of a habit and she'll just ask for silly wands or tickly wands so she likes to be playful and me to make her laugh, so we have a very good relationship.'
(Gay father)

It was clear from some interviews that a positive relationship took time to achieve and that the process wasn't always easy.

'Yeah I think we are close, we're very fond of each other and [child]'s showing that more and more. It took a little while for [child] to be able to do that, to warm to us as well, you know, to have deep feelings, I guess, but yes it's there now and she can be very affectionate, which is lovely.'
(Heterosexual mother)

'Very well, when he first moved in I found it so difficult and now I look back and I'm astonished at how hard I found it 'cause now, it's not always easy and it has made me – I used to think I was very tolerant and patient and I'm not, I'm intolerant and very impatient [laughs] which is a bit sad 'cause it can affect your view of yourself but I think we've got a very good relationship.'
(Heterosexual mother)

Some parents felt their relationships with their children involved a mixture of both positivity and difficulty.

'We have a good relationship, earlier in the placement it was a little more tricky. He's got a tendency to focus on like one person particularly and early on in the placement he kind of flitted between [partner] and me and I think that's just something that he'd learned from previous experiences really, and that's something he still does now sometimes with his friends but he kind of focuses on one person and they're the best person, sometimes exclusively to other people. It's less so now that he's more settled and we're

understanding more about that but it still pops up sometimes.'
(Gay father)

'Pretty well, I mean, she certainly has some very challenging aspects to her personality and I'm certainly not the parent I would like to be with [child]. I've had to adapt my parenting style to parent her, I'm not as laid back, I'm quite a laid back person but I'm not as laid back as I'd like to be and I find I have to overly manage her, which I find quite difficult and a bit tedious really ... But I think we do get on really well actually.'
(Lesbian mother)

'I think I get along with him fine now. I think it's been a really difficult long journey and sometimes I think you know it's quite difficult, because [child] is quite difficult in terms of his behaviour and just parenting him in general. I know I don't get the same rewards from him as I do from the other two [siblings] and that can sometimes be quite difficult, and I'm aware of that, you know with [child] it's hard work and the rewards are few and far between but then you treasure them and they become more precious you know, so I think ... I mean God, we've made so much progress, you know, when I think back to how our relationship used to be.'
(Heterosexual mother)

A minority of parents recognised that they were still experiencing difficulties and that building on their relationships with the children was a long process that would take time.

'Yeah, I still don't think I've got to the stage of that rush of emotional love about her but I suspect there's more than I think. It's so hard to quantify, it's such an artificial situation. It's quite sporadic, my biggest surprise was that it was quite hard for me to make an attachment to them. Nobody talks about "You may not love

them ..." You know, everyone just assumes it's going to happen and, you know, I've talked to quite a few adoptive parents where it hasn't and I'm just hoping that it's accumulative.'
(Heterosexual mother)

'On good days very well [laughs], I think he doubts my motives the most ... I think it's probably, well, our counsellor thinks that he's kind of put me in the mother role in his head. He's decided – I mean he knows perfectly well that I'm his dad but it's me he associates with the roles his mum did ... 'cause his mum's the one that did the abuse, I think he finds it harder to trust me. I'm also more of the disciplinarian so it's me ... He finds it hard – he will look at my face for signs of disapproval and things like that.'
(Gay father)

Parents also discussed how comfortable both their children and they felt with giving and receiving affection from one another. Some parents described it as effortless.

'We'll have a hug or ... what she does do actually when she's in the car is – it's probably a silly thing but when I'm in the car driving and they're obviously in the back, they usually watch a film or something but she just gives me a thumbs up and she gives the best thumbs up in the world, and if you can have an affectionate thumbs up, it's the best thumbs up in the world you can give and someone might say yeah, alright, but it's really distinctive and when she gives me that thumbs up I know she's really happy.'
(Heterosexual father)

'Hugs, she'll often ask for a hug, at night time we have sort of special kisses before she goes to sleep where I sort of, you know, we rub noses and that sort of thing, the sort of thing that I had from my mum when I was little.'
(Gay father)

'Of course he's very cuddly and we're both very touchy feely and I say, "Oh, I love getting cuddles from you," so he knows he can do that. At weekends he'll climb into our bed for cuddles and tickles and things like that.'
(Gay father)

Other parents reported that this was something that didn't come without difficulty and often developed over time.

'She doesn't give affection very easily, I was the only one she'd cuddle for months and months. It's taken her a very long time to be cuddled.'
(Lesbian mother)

'That's something that we kind of worked on 'cause he was placed with us when he was 11 months old and his foster carers at the time described him as not being a very cuddly baby and we noticed that he wasn't, so we've deliberately tried to be affectionate and we have family hugs like every day and he's really taken to that so he understands about kissing and cuddling and things like that.'
(Lesbian mother)

'Yeah, I didn't at first because she didn't and that's what's difficult to begin with is, I got nothing back so, you know, I'd give her her bottle and as soon as she's finished she'd just get up and go and that's very very difficult and it's very difficult to be doing all the hard work of being a parent and getting nothing back. But now we're very affectionate, yeah. I mean she – this is the thing – she never used to need affection but now she is amazingly affectionate. So, for a start, she will come to me when she needs me and get into bed with me, stroke my arms and cuddle me, and so now she's completely able to say I need a cuddle and to access that physical affection.'
(Lesbian mother)

> Overall, the quality and characteristics of the parent–child relationship were very similar across all three family types, and the majority of parents were content with their relationship with their child. Parents from all three family types were dedicated to developing good relationships with their children, no matter what difficulties they faced, with many reporting profound improvements in comparison to how they were at placement.

8 Family life

Parents were also asked about their day-to-day routines with their children, to get an impression of family life.

Routines

There were no significant differences between family types in terms of bedtime and morning routines. The majority of parents experienced no difficulty or only minor reluctance when it came to their child's morning routine (gay fathers 93 per cent, lesbian mothers 77.5 per cent and heterosexual parents 84 per cent). Similarly, only a few families experienced difficulties when putting their child to bed, with no gay fathers and only 10 per cent of lesbian mothers and 14 per cent of heterosexual parents reporting significant reluctance or major battles.

Child care

Gay fathers, lesbian mothers and heterosexual parents accessed similar levels of child care, with 45 per cent of the children in each family type looked after regularly by others. This was, on average, for five hours a week, although children in gay father families had slightly more child care, at seven hours on average. Gay fathers were more likely to use childminders, whereas lesbian mothers and heterosexual parents used afterschool clubs or relatives/friends.

Parents' roles

There were no differences between family types in the roles parents assumed; parents divided childcare responsibilities almost identically.

In each family type there was usually a primary caregiver (Parent A). In heterosexual families the primary caregiver was nearly always the mother, who was less likely to be working full-time than the primary caregiver in same-sex families. Approximately 20 per cent of the couples in each family type shared childcare evenly. This low percentage is rather surprising with regards to same-sex parents, who are usually viewed as somewhat more egalitarian in their parenting roles.

Parents were asked how satisfied they were with the division of childcare responsibilities and again, no differences were found between family types. Among Parent As, 83 per cent of gay fathers, 70 per cent of lesbian mothers and 68 per cent of heterosexual mothers reported being mostly to very satisfied with their current arrangements. Similar satisfaction was expressed by Parent Bs, with 69 per cent of gay fathers, 59 per cent of lesbian mothers and 80 per cent of heterosexual fathers reporting being mostly to very satisfied with the division of childcare.

All parents assumed fairly traditional patterns of parenting responsibilities, with no differences between family types. Thus, it appears that family life is very similar for children, regardless of parents' sexual orientation.

9 Becoming a parent: the journey to adoption

Parents were asked about their reasons for wanting to become parents and why and how they decided to adopt.

Many gay fathers, lesbian mothers and heterosexual parents gave similar accounts of having a strong desire to become a parent.

'I've known since I was 12 that I was going to have kids.'
(Gay father)

'I think right on maybe our third date or something [partner] said I do want children, you know that, if this is going anywhere further that's going to happen, so that was always going there.'
(Lesbian mother)

'I think I did just decide that I really needed to have children, it was kind of that thing of probably ... getting towards 30 I suppose and thinking ... I'd better do this if I'm going to do it.'
(Heterosexual mother)

Families of all types looked for the fulfilment that having children could bring.

'I suppose we were looking for a way to add meaning to what we were doing.'
(Lesbian mother)

'We didn't used to go out much, but we did have nice holidays, you know, we've been to most parts of the world, but I think even that got a bit ... we'd done that [laughs]! It was time to do something else then and we both ... were of the same mind that ... we'd both like to have children.'
(Heterosexual father)

For many, this was also shaped by reaching the right point in their lives.

'Well, we talked about it for ... quite some time ago while we were living in [city] and we were both working very long hours ... it just wasn't practical. Then we relocated, we moved here. And about a year or so after we moved, we started thinking about it again; we decided now that the time was right.'
(Gay father)

Compared to heterosexual parents, fewer same-sex couples, particularly gay fathers, expected that they would become parents one day; many had viewed their sexual identity as incompatible with parenthood.

'I always presumed I'd be a dad, and one of the hardest things to come to terms with about being gay was the assumption that I wouldn't have children.'
(Gay father)

The experience of growing up gay and the effect it had on expectations of future family life was particularly salient for the older parents in the study.

'Never thought I would have children anyway, you know, when you come out [...] when I was in my 20s I didn't even think ... that was not even an option in my mind and marriage, it was all just sort of ... thought you'd have a series of relationships like everybody else did, and you might be lucky and sort of have somebody that stayed around for a period of time, but this ... I mean this is a different period of life that we're living now than I would have ever thought we would, so I think we're very lucky.'
(Lesbian mother)

15

Parents discussed how various influences transformed their ideas and led them to contemplate forming families. For some, this included overcoming their own concerns about same-sex parenting.

> 'We started off in honesty saying well, we ought to see whether we are suitable, it may not be the right thing, it may not be the right thing for a child in particular because we clearly would be an unusual family and whether that's the right thing to do. And it took us quite a while to come to the conclusion that we potentially were good parents ... and actually could offer quite a lot to a child, although we'd inherently be bringing a difference to that child ... the number of kids in care that there are, that probably was of lesser importance than the value that we could bring.'
> (Gay father)

For others, having always wanted to parent but never knowing how, the legislative change that enabled joint adoption by same-sex couples was all that was necessary to help couples pursue parenthood.

> 'But we'd talked about it for years, but always in the sort of abstract and then of course the law changed. Which then meant that, you know, being a same-sex couple couldn't be ... a barrier to it. And we'd succeed or fail on our own merits after that point, and then it was kind of like, well, we shall ... shall we give it a go.'
> (Gay father)

Once the couples decided that they would like to have children together, they then had to decide how to go about it. For the majority of heterosexual couples, this was fairly straightforward; it was taken as a given that they would try for biological children, and the idea that they might not have biological children simply was not considered.

> 'I mean if we could have naturally had children that would have been the obvious [...] it's just what you kind of automatically would probably do, do you know what I mean, like ... and I mean now I kind of think God, why would you do it that way, you know, now that's what I'd think. But at the time it's just ... you get married and you just think you'll have a baby.'
> (Heterosexual mother)

While attempting to have a biological child is an obvious option for heterosexual couples, lesbian mothers and, especially, gay fathers have fewer reproductive opportunities available. While lesbian mothers can attempt to become pregnant using donor sperm, gay fathers must enlist the help of an egg donor and surrogate mother; the latter is much more difficult in terms of cost, availability and legal protection. This difference in the availability of reproductive opportunities is reflected in family type differences in the journeys to parenthood.

Tried to conceive a child unsuccessfully

The vast majority of heterosexual couples had attempted, unsuccessfully, to have biological children before adopting, while 15 lesbian mother couples had also tried, unsuccessfully, to conceive children. Gay fathers were markedly different from both groups in that only one gay father couple had tried to conceive a child through surrogacy prior to adopting.

For many heterosexual couples, not being able to have a child through natural conception took parents on a "typical journey" to adoption following infertility.

> 'I dunno, we got to the point where it wasn't happening normally and we ... I guess there's a fairly standard pattern of, if it isn't happening normally, then you try a bit of IVF, and if that doesn't work then you think about

Figure 6: Tried to conceive a child unsuccessfully

	Gay fathers	Lesbian mothers	Heterosexual parents
Yes	2%	38%	90%
No	98%	62%	10%

other options, and that's when we started thinking about adoption.'
(Heterosexual father)

Many heterosexual parents experienced stress and loss along the way to parenthood as multiple rounds of fertility treatment failed or they experienced miscarriages, and, for some, bereavement after babies were born. For many, moving on to adoption was a positive choice and an end to a very difficult period of invasive treatments and upsetting experiences.

'So the IVF didn't work and we tried two or three times and I was doing ... maybe the third time I was starting to take the drugs and realised that I absolutely didn't want to be pregnant because of all the worry that we'd gone through with these two ones failing. I thought if I actually was to get pregnant it would just make me a bit mad because I'd be worried the entire way through the whole pregnancy that something would go wrong, and I'd just had enough, so we gave up mid-way through an IVF cycle, which is quite a positive way to stop, because it was us stopping as opposed to running out of options, and yeah, so I just rang [partner] and said I'm not going to do it and all this over the phone, don't want to do it, let's adopt, and he said OK.'
(Heterosexual mother)

A similar journey was undertaken by some of the lesbian mothers, who had experienced fertility problems when they tried to conceive using donor sperm.

'I tried to have a child of my own. I had one miscarriage, I had gynaecological problems, I tried for about five years after I miscarried, so ongoing fertility stuff so [adoption] wasn't my first choice. I know a lot of lesbians and gays say it was their first choice, but it wasn't my first choice, I wanted my own child.'
(Lesbian mother)

However, for many lesbian mothers and nearly all gay fathers, adoption was the preferred route to parenthood – a key difference between heterosexual and same-sex couples. This may be because same-sex couples already doubt that they will become biological parents, and so reflect more on the meaning of having biological children.

'Maybe this is more of a characteristic of being in a gay relationship, but we didn't feel a need for them to have our DNA in a way that maybe some straight couples would. And you know, maybe I felt a little less bound by society in that respect. I think when straight couples don't have children and are looking for children, their first focus always seems to be, and maybe we're being a little unfair, but the vast majority of the time, is try to have your own kids hard. Whereas for us, I mean that was never going to happen. We thought, you know, trying to find a way to make it possible for us to have children with one of our DNA through surrogacy or anything like that just seemed kind of irrelevant.'

(Gay father)

Preferred route to parenthood

All parents were specifically asked about their preferences regarding adoption and their responses were coded into one of three categories: whether adoption was their first port of call and first preference, whether alternative routes were considered or attempted but adopting was of equal preference, or whether parents preferred to have children via means other than adoption. Gay fathers were significantly more likely to report that adoption was their first choice, heterosexual couples preferred to have children via other routes or found adoption equally preferable and lesbian mothers fell between the two groups.

While some heterosexual parents came to adoption after fertility treatments, others were open to adopting either from the outset or as soon as they realised they could not conceive naturally. Reasons for this included discomfort with, or religious objections to, fertility treatment

or concerns about the stress and pressure fertility treatment might put on them as a couple or individuals. Discomfort with the idea of using donor gametes, and awareness of advancing age and a need to decide which option would offer them the best chance of parenthood, also prompted parents to think about adoption.

'We thought about egg donation, but we decided that maybe wasn't right, it wasn't right for us anyway... so then I suppose we started thinking more along the lines of adoption, you know, before we were too old and too over the hill!'
(Heterosexual father)

Openness to adoption was also associated with having prior familiarity with adoption.

'My dad's adopted, and my aunt's adopted, and actually quite a few of my cousins as well, so adoption is a ... you know, familiar theme in our family. So you know, it's not something I was ever that uncomfortable with. And yeah, then we found out definitely, absolutely never would we ever be able to conceive, so I was kind of like OK, that's it, the plan B was very much a positive alternative for us.'
(Heterosexual mother)

Figure 7: Preferred route to parenthood

	Gay fathers	Lesbian mothers	Heterosexual parents
Alternatives preferred	2%	15%	49%
Considered/attempted alternatives but adoption equal preference	15%	30%	43%
Always preferred adoption	83%	55%	8%

And for many heterosexual parents the moral argument for adoption helped them to decide to adopt. Wanting to help children in need was the key reason given by the parents who chose to adopt as a first choice, usually after they had had biological children earlier on.

> 'We just thought it might be ... rather than have another child of our own, that it might be ... nice to adopt a child. Help someone a bit less fortunate than ourselves – do you know what I mean?'
> (Heterosexual father)

Interestingly, while some heterosexual parents had always wanted to adopt, they had tried to conceive a child first. For three families, this was prompted by those they contacted about adoption.

> 'We went on holiday to Africa when we were newly married, saw lots of orphans out there, decided we would come home and adopt. We were living in [English town] at the time. We went to the local authority and asked them if we could adopt and they said, "No, go away, you're far too young, go away and have your own children first and then come back to us in ten years' time." So we tried to have our own children and couldn't, and then ended up adopting.'
> (Heterosexual mother)

For same-sex couples, not wanting biological children or, in the case of lesbian mothers, not wanting to go through pregnancy and childbirth was a main reason for adopting.

> 'Neither of us had that great urge, or that great maternal instinct to give birth, neither of us have ever shared that feeling that you need to produce your own. Adoption is a perfectly natural choice if you don't care about giving birth. You want to nurture a life, which I think is what we did want to do. We were quite clear about what we wanted and

what we wanted to do with that. So I think if you're quite clear about that then it's ... the decision is made for you really.'
> (Lesbian mother)

For some, particularly for gay fathers considering surrogacy, the decision not to have biological children was discussed in moral terms.

> 'Once we'd talked about being parents, this was the only thing we were really interested in because we didn't want to create another child so ... with children needing adoption, that was the only thing ... that was the only option that we seriously considered really, we didn't want to do anything else.'
> (Gay father)

As same-sex partners inevitably rely on third parties to conceive children, the concerns same-sex couples held about the roles third parties would play were a key reason for favouring adoption.

> 'We've come with a no for everything else, because surrogacy doesn't work for two men, in my opinion, because whoever the birth mother is, you can't just exclude them and then expect a child as they grow up to understand why that person has been excluded. It just doesn't work, so then you're involving that person and what level do you involve that person in? If we want to be the parents, then we want to be the parents, you know.'
> (Gay father)

Despite adoption sometimes involving the birth family through contact, it was still seen by many as a less complex arrangement. In particular, at the time many of these couples adopted, adoption provided much surer legal rights for parents (i.e. both legal parents) than conception involving a surrogate.

Beyond legal equality as parents, same-sex parents favoured adoption because it provided the unique advantage that neither parent was biologically related to the child. The desire for complete equality of parenting rights and relationships was a key reason same-sex couples favoured adoption.

'Friends who have had a biological child ... everyone is obsessed to know which one is the real mother, which, you know, makes one of them more the mother than the other one. It's just really nice to have that be completely shared, and we are absolutely fully equal as far as that goes.'
(Lesbian mother)

For heterosexual, gay and lesbian families, the reasons for adopting were complex and overlapping. For all families, the underlying reason was the desire to be parents and to love and be loved by children. While adoption provided an opportunity for these couples to become parents, for same-sex couples, adoption came with the additional advantages of providing equality in the absence of a genetic connection to the child and a potentially more straightforward family form than co-parenting or third party donation. Also, same-sex couples were less concerned about biological parenthood than heterosexual couples. This made adoption the first choice for many gay men and lesbians.

10 Openness in adoption

Structural openness

Parents were asked how much contact their child had with their birth family in the past 12 months and whether this was face-to-face contact or letterbox contact, or whether they did not have any contact.

Child's contact in the past 12 months

Around half of the children in all family types had some form of contact with their birth mothers. There was no significant difference among family types in how much contact there was with the child's birth mother.

A noticeably smaller percentage of children (20–28%) had contact with their birth fathers, again with no difference among family types. It is interesting to note that gay fathers were more likely to have a contact arrangement in place with birth fathers: 64 per cent of gay fathers, 54 per cent of lesbian mothers and 33 per cent of heterosexual parents had contact arrangements agreed with the birth father. And as can be seen in Figure 8, only 20 per cent of gay fathers' children actually had contact, compared to 64 per cent who had contact arrangements in place. So birth fathers may be less likely to maintain contact arrangements with children placed with gay fathers. However, it was not possible to ascertain the cause from our data, as there were many other factors that influenced whether contact is maintained.

Children were more likely to have contact with their birth siblings and to have this face-to-face rather than by letterbox, compared to contact with their birth parents. There was no difference between family types in whether contact arrangements with birth siblings were being fulfilled.

Overall, children in all three family types experienced similar levels of contact with their birth families.

Parent's feelings regarding birth family contact

Parents were asked how they felt about their child's contact with their birth family, and

Figure 8: Contact child has received in the past 12 months

	Gay fathers		Lesbian mothers		Heterosexual parents	
	Arranged	Received	Arranged	Received	Arranged	Received
Birth mother:						
Face-to-face	2%	2%	5%	5%	12%	12%
Letterbox	78%	44%	72%	41%	59%	35%
None	20%	54%	23%	54%	29%	53%
Birth father:						
Face-to-face	0%	0%	8%	8%	9%	9%
Letterbox	64%	20%	46%	20%	24%	16%
None	36%	80%	46%	72%	67%	75%
Birth siblings:						
Face-to-face	47%	47%	44%	44%	32%	30%
Letterbox	34%	19%	24%	18%	25%	19%
None	19%	34%	32%	38%	43%	51%

responses were coded as positive, neutral, ambivalent or concerned.

As can be seen from Figure 9, the majority of all parents felt positive or neutral about their child's contact with his or her birth family. No difference in feelings about contact was found among family types.

Some parents were supportive of birth family contact, expressing positivity and feeling it was significant for their child.

'I think it's important, I think it will be important to him as an adult, I don't think it's important to him now particularly. I think in a way he'd prefer not to think about it or not to talk about it ... but I understand its purpose and I think when he's older he will appreciate those letters.'
(Gay father)

'I think it's great. I mean we were lucky enough to meet her birth mum. We've not met birth dad, but we'd love to, and that's something I think that the post-adoption team are still trying to work towards, because I think it's just important for [child] to really kind of get that ... these are the people that gave birth to you. And we're lucky in lots of ways that their story is ... it's not got cruelty in the background, it's not got drug abuse, they're just ... a pair of unfortunate people really who can't quite look after themselves, let alone children. So I think it was harder for the other children that were taken into care, but with [child] and [sibling], they were both put into care pretty much from birth.'
(Gay father)

'I think with the sister – the older sister – I think it's absolutely brilliant and the older

sister fought very hard for it and we did for [child] 'cause [child] has an amazing memory and remembers so much about her and she cared for him a lot, so he was more attached to her than [birth] mum, so I think that's brilliant. I think it's good for the sister and I think it's good for [child].'
(Lesbian mother)

'I think that it's probably a positive thing. I mean it's a little bit difficult and a little bit scary, you know, when it's actually going to happen but I think that, I mean my feeling is that it's a positive thing that it takes away the question that – I think it's important in terms of their identity as they get older. Just in terms of getting information ... when she was younger and when she first came here I think it was very important for her to know that she was going to see them again and that I was kind of looking after that for her. So yeah, in general, positive feelings around it, although it's something that I also have difficult feelings around as well.'
(Heterosexual mother)

Other parents felt that contact with the birth family would be worthwhile, but only if it were to be consistent and appropriate, otherwise it would only cause problems for their child.

'I think it's a great thing to do as long as it works. If [birth] mum's going to keep her side of the deal and reply regularly writing letters with appropriate content, I think it's a very positive thing. If we can't rely on hearing back, then I would prefer not to have it because I don't think it's fair on the children for them to write letters and not be sure if they're going to get anything back. So we have to feel a certain level of confidence that we're going to get something in return and that it's going to be appropriate. You know, really it's whatever's in her best interests. So if it can work in her best interests then all

well and good, but if not, then I'm not going to do it just because we've been told we have to do it.'
(Gay father)

'There have been a few letters where, you know, it's all about dumping their guilt, really – this whole thing about, you know, "Miss you every day" – and that kind of gets me thinking, well, if you miss them that much, you would actually have got your life together to make sure they stayed with you. And I think, well, actually it's really unfair to put that on two little girls. And so, you know, we have sent things back because we've thought they were inappropriate and have been very clear with social services about what we will accept and what we won't. So as I say, there's things like that, but in the main everything that comes is given to them and they put the cards up with everybody else's cards and pictures of [biological brother] are around the house, so it's not a big secret and it's not

... they don't have to choose, they don't have to feel as if they are being disloyal to us, because you know they're not.'
(Lesbian mother)

'It would just upset them and ... and if it then doesn't continue because then they're aware that they can write to her next February, and they'll write to her, but if then nothing comes back, you get a rejection cycle again, don't you?'
(Gay father)

Some parents experienced mixed feelings about contact with their child's birth family, with some finding it difficult.

'Sometimes it's hard because you forget. We're that close now and they're that settled that it really does sometimes feel like they've been with us forever and sometimes I honestly forget that they've got this other family and they've had this other life. And so

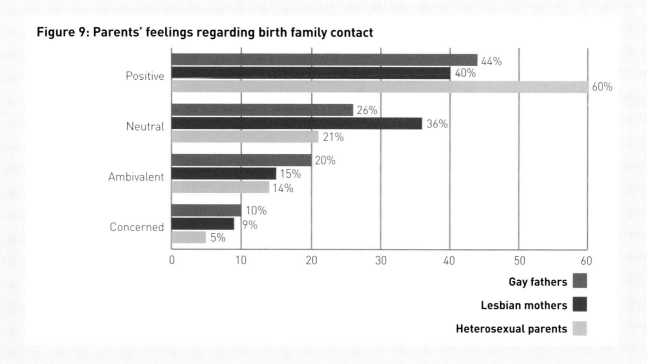

Figure 9: Parents' feelings regarding birth family contact

Positive — Gay fathers 44%, Lesbian mothers 40%, Heterosexual parents 60%

Neutral — Gay fathers 26%, Lesbian mothers 36%, Heterosexual parents 21%

Ambivalent — Gay fathers 20%, Lesbian mothers 15%, Heterosexual parents 14%

Concerned — Gay fathers 10%, Lesbian mothers 9%, Heterosexual parents 5%

Gay fathers
Lesbian mothers
Heterosexual parents

when they talk about it, it kind of just brings that back up that there's been so much that we've missed and there's so much that we don't know about, so sometimes it stings a little bit. But at the same time we would never stop them from talking about it or losing that identity because we know it's really really important – it's like if they've got pictures of their siblings, we know it's important to say, "Oh look, don't you look the same, you've got the same eyes, you've got the same mouth," because they need that identity that they look like somebody.'
(Lesbian mother)

'It's a tricky one 'cause I don't like contact. I always get a bit emotional and anxious about it because it brings up the realisation – you know, you go about your everyday business without really thinking so much that they're adopted as such, they're just part of the family. And then you're sort of struck with it once a year and you kind of have to, you know, address it and write it and you can't help but think about the things that happened before the children were removed and, you know, it's hard. I wouldn't want any more 'cause, you know, I'm not their foster carer, I'm their dad now and I don't want to feel like I'm caring for them for someone else.'
(Gay father)

> There were mixed feelings surrounding birth family contact, often dependent on the child's experiences with their birth families pre-adoption. However, these feelings did not differ according to family type.

Communicative openness

Parents were asked questions about whether they had spoken to their child about being adopted. Nearly all families had had conversations with their children about their birth history and adoption.

Only two gay father families, one lesbian mother family and one heterosexual parent family had not yet discussed adoption with their children. This was either because the child had developmental delay and thus would not understand fully, or because the parents felt their child was too young and intended to broach the subject when they were older.

No differences were found between family types with respect to how often parents discussed adoption with their children. Frequencies varied depending on whether the topic arose a lot because of contact arrangements with the children's birth families, or because children were asking questions, or it was just not being discussed so frequently at the time of the study.

Parents also gave details about what they discussed with their child about adoption.

'Well, she's asking questions about – we call them "tummy mummy" and "tummy daddy"– about why she was put into care, why couldn't they look after her. We talk about "bad medicine" – that they took "bad medicine", we talk about that they weren't able to give them what they needed to make them safe and to feed them. We say that nobody taught them how to do it, so they weren't able to. They're asking a lot more questions now and of course when they see their siblings it reminds them – they see them three times a year – they're all older, you know, two are not but ... and they ask questions about their elder sibling that they don't see now – she looked after them and that's a big issue for them, not seeing her.'
(Lesbian mother)

'We use the word "adoption". We haven't gone into detail about what that means. You know, we've said you were inside mummy L's tummy and she loves you very much but she wasn't able to look after you, so then you went to your foster carer, and then you came to live with us. We wanted a little girl and we decided we could look after you. So we talk about it in those terms. She doesn't fully understand what adoption means, but she knows she has a mummy L and she talks about her from time to time.'
(Gay father)

'There's a book, *My New Family*, and we've gone through that a couple of times, and sometimes she'll want it and she'll ask a question and we'll go through it. So she knows that [foster carer] was her foster carer because we describe it as ... [birth mother] couldn't look after you, so [foster carer] looked after you until ... whilst your forever mummy and daddy (i.e. "Mummy" and "Daddy") could be found and then we came along.'
(Heterosexual father)

Parents also indicated that their adopted children's life story books were very helpful in explaining their birth histories and journeys to adoption.

'We'll just, like, read his life story work with him ... he knows that he was not born from my tummy and he's sort of becoming a little bit more aware of it now ... You go through a phase of reading his life story book like most evenings for maybe a week or so, and then nothing again for another month or six weeks or something like that.'
(Heterosexual mother)

'He has a life story book which is in his bedroom and pretty much he can pick it up and look at it on his own. And he did the other day ... this was a very personal moment for [child] actually ... but he did the other day pick it up and go through and work out this is important.'
(Heterosexual father)

'I mean we look in the birth story book and we look at pictures of [birth parents] and these sorts of things, but we've not gone into the full sort of ins and outs. But I think it's better to kind of leave the information there for her and then, when she's ready to access it, she can talk to us about it completely openly and we can talk about it then. But all the information's there in the life story book for her.'
(Gay father)

There were no family type differences with respect to how comfortable parents felt discussing adoption with their children; around 80 per cent of parents in all family types felt completely comfortable.

How parents felt about discussing adoption with their children did not affect the frequency of conversations; parents would continue to engage in discussions despite any difficulties encountered.

Wanting to be open and honest with their children was a common theme in the parents' descriptions of their feelings about these discussions.

'I feel it's important for them to understand where they're from. I mean I'm happy that they talk about it because that means they feel safe and comfortable with us really.'
(Heterosexual father)

'Well, I think, it's a fact of life and I want them to be realistic about it and I want them to feel that they can say anything, ask anything, that I won't be offended or hurt by them wanting to ... I want them to know as much as possible. I want them to feel they can ask anything.'
(Gay father)

'I feel quite pleased to be able to discuss it. You know, it's certainly not something that I ever wanted to "hush-hush". We're quite open about it, I mean they were four and five when they moved in, so it's never been a secret.'
(Heterosexual mother)

Some parents reported finding these discussions quite hard, for different reasons.

'Really emotional. A lot of different emotions. Just sort of ... just, you know, so happy that she is in our family I suppose, but sad for the birth family. Anxious I suppose about what the future holds, and how she will feel about it when she's older, and just anxious to try and make everything as positive as possible, really. I don't want her to feel bad about it for any reason.'
(Lesbian mother)

'I perhaps sometimes don't really want to acknowledge the fact that he's adopted, I wish he was mine, my biological ... so yeah ... but it is, I'm very conscious that it's something that we need to be very open about, you know, so that he is prepared for the future and knows as much as possible.'
(Heterosexual mother)

Parents also reported difficulties in knowing how and when to discuss the more traumatic aspects of their child's birth histories.

'It's an important thing to do, I don't get anxious about it, I just feel like ... because there's a context here which is quite difficult, I'm not sure how and when to explain about the drug use aspect. For some reason I find it easier to talk about the violence aspect, because it's something that children can relate to in terms of, well, they did see the violence. I don't know how aware they are of the drug use and so that's something that is going ... I don't really know when to approach that and how to approach it.'
(Lesbian mother)

Parents often expressed the desire to discuss their children's birth histories and adoption with them in the right way.

'I don't know that I feel anything untoward. I feel ... what do I feel ... I feel ... I hope ... my feeling is that I hope I'm doing it right, I hope I am explaining and I hope I'm not making it too complicated. And I suppose I have some anxieties around how I explain it because I tend to make leaps for them that maybe they haven't quite caught up with, and I think that's what I feel. I think that's my overriding feeling, you know, the feeling of wanting to do it right so that they understand.'
(Heterosexual mother)

'Fine, I feel I need to be fairly careful … it's tricky isn't it … I don't want to get it wrong … but I don't want him to feel like it's … mostly that I feel I want to get it right, I want him to feel comfortable with it.'
(Heterosexual mother)

Overall, parents in all types of families recognised the importance of open dialogue about adoption and birth history.

'It's not that long ago that it would be seen as a bit of a taboo. Whereas nowadays I think it's – because children in general are so accepting of things – I think it would ultimately cause you more problems if you tried to steer away from it or just sort of gloss over something. It would just sort of build up to the extent that when they got older to really start questioning you, I think it would really just build up more resentment. Whereas if you've drip-fed them throughout the years, because you can have a conversation or talk to them about something, and it's not as if he continues and he wants more and more. He'll say something, you'll have a chat, and that's it, he moves on.'
(Heterosexual father)

Parents in all three family types discussed their children's histories in similar manners and frequencies, with a very high level of openness.

11 Children's experiences with same-sex parents

The majority of same-sex parents felt it was important to have conversations with their children about their family type, with 91 per cent of gay and lesbian parents having had conversations with their children about having two mums or two dads.

> 'We've always talked to them. It's not something that can be hidden away, and it's not something you should hide away because then that makes it that the kids might feel ashamed about it so, it's something that you need to discuss and be open about.'
> (Lesbian mother)

When this hadn't yet been discussed, parents explained that their child had developmental delay or learning difficulties and so would struggle to understand, or they felt their child was too young but planned to begin talking about it as the child grew older.

The frequency of these discussions varied, with some parents reporting a higher frequency when their child was initially placed and fewer discussions as their child got older. Many parents reported that older children, in particular, accepted their family as it was, but felt that their child knew the subject was never off limits if they needed to ask something.

> 'Not very often at all now, I think maybe earlier on it would have done because he was getting used to it and explaining it and them understanding it, but it's normalised now, they don't think anything of it.'
> (Gay father)

In these discussions, parents reported talking about different types of families. This was to illustrate that there are lots of different families in the world, not just their own.

> 'We just say it's normal. And we give examples of the fact that children live in all sorts of families, one of my nieces lives with her gran. Four of our nieces and nephews are dual heritage and they're Muslim and we're not. You know, diversity is everywhere, you can't escape it and actually why would you want to? Embrace it because it makes family life more rich. And so we've always kind of talked about the fact that there's nothing two dads can't do that a mum and a dad can do or two mums can do. Just that it might be done slightly differently.'
> (Gay father)

> 'Well, we've just explained things, that there are different relationships, that some … some people have mothers and fathers, some people have mothers … have two mothers, and some people have two fathers and so on, so we talk about different family relationships.'
> (Gay father)

They also explained that two people of the same sex can love each other.

> 'We sort of discuss about it being more important to love somebody and be loved back than whether it's … you're fitting in with what other people do.'
> (Lesbian mother)

> 'We talked about it in a way that it's just about two people who love each other.'
> (Lesbian mother)

> 'We sort of say it doesn't matter who you fall in love with. Anybody can get married, whether it's two girls or two boys or a boy and a girl, it doesn't matter.'
> (Lesbian mother)

To help children understand gay and lesbian relationships in an age-appropriate manner, parents often read books to their children featuring same-sex parents.

'There's a really good book about boys adopted by a gay couple and it's fantastic – it is [child]'s life. That's really good for [child] now to have a big book of families, it's superb – and it's just about families coming in all shapes and sizes – and he knows that.'
(Gay father)

Parents often introduced these books to their children's schools and nurseries.

'So we've taken books up in the past to nursery so that those children have had a story, which are stories we've used with him. You know, sort of *Tango Makes Three* is probably one of the more appropriate ones. We've got *King and King*, and *King and King* … I dunno if it's called *Go on Holiday*, but they adopt a child so … and then we've got a book about somebody's party, which is about all sorts of diverse families and so it brings in again, just as one of the families, there's a same-sex couple in there as well. So we sort of use those … give those as resources for other people to use as well.'
(Gay father)

They generally reported satisfaction with the attitudes of school staff.

'This time last year we did a piece in [a newspaper], it was like a double page spread for BAAF for National Adoption Week, and the teacher used that, saw it and you know, with permission used it to have a discussion in [child]'s class that day about all the different family structures. And they all talked about the different family structures, you know, because it is the sort of community where there aren't many normal family structures,

if you know what I mean! So that was quite good that they were all able to discuss it so he's fully aware I think there.'
(Gay father)

'So on Father's Day they make cards for my dad and that kind of thing, and school is aware and they deal with it appropriately.'
(Lesbian mother)

Many families met with other same-sex families, either as friends or as part of LGBT groups, so that children could realise that they are not alone.

'And we meet up, they have a family day … we don't think we should be isolated, we're already in the [regional] adoption group, but we felt that we should do just for the boys' sake so that when we go to things they can see there's other children who've got two mummies or two daddies, so we tend to go – they have three a year, we go to one a year, make sure we do one and it does help, it definitely did 'cause they could see, "Oh, you know that little boy has got two mummies as well," "Yeah yeah, you know a lot of children do," and it was like … it just helps a little bit.'
(Lesbian mother)

'I mean we're lucky we've got friends, there's another two – a couple who used to live just round the corner, they've just moved, they've got three boys who they've adopted, so you know [child] and [sibling] can also see another family with two gay men as the parents. And we've got our friends – a lesbian couple who are hoping to have children – so they're kind of already seeing these diverse families as well.'
(Gay father)

Are children with same-sex parents bullied?

Of the 59 children who were interviewed, none reported being teased about having gay or lesbian parents. Parents were also asked about whether they were aware of any homophobic bullying directed towards their child. Four children with gay fathers and three children with lesbian mothers were reported to have experienced homophobia of some kind from their peers. It is important to note that just seven out of a possible 81 families reported that their children were teased about their same-sex parents.

Below are some examples of what parents reported as having been said to their children.

'You're different 'cause you've got two dads.'

'It's stupid and nasty to have two dads.'

'I'm going to get my dad to come and shoot your dad!'

'They're not your real mums.'

'Your mums are lesbians!'

When inappropriate comments had been made to their children, parents felt satisfied with the action of the school and/or the other parents.

'We spoke to the teacher about it and she was very supportive. They have a counselling system there and she and I spoke again last time when he got out of school and I have to say they are great, they're really really good at being aware of that and keeping me up to date.'
(Gay father)

'I spoke to her mother, and her mother was devastated and she had a word with her, and she apologised to [child] the next day.'
(Gay father)

Same-sex parents reported initial concerns that their children might face homophobic reactions from other children.

'It's a great irony that that was a huge worry that we had, right from when we were doing all that agonising about should we, shouldn't we. And actually it's been the least significant issue. I mean, I don't think we're naive about the fact that it probably will become ... But so far, they're invited to all the children's parties that you'd expect them to be. I don't think ... In fact, if anything, it has made us more interesting to people, in that slightly, you know, people do like a little bit of, "Oh, really? How interesting!" '
(Lesbian mother)

'I'm not aware that she's ever been teased, but it's something I am really conscious of though, and it was a big part of my kind of worry initially about adopting.'
(Lesbian mother)

Although the majority of parents reported that they felt their child was not bullied, some did say that their child faced questions about their family.

'I'd say, you know, that the children are completely accepting of it and I'd think the adults that we've come across ... I'd say the only thing probably is that as he's got older, people have maybe got more curious about the situation, but not in a negative way and have maybe just been trying to make sense of it in terms of – it's not really

about why he's got two dads, it's more where's his mum, that might be the kind of thing that might come up, rather than about focusing on the two dads. I think it's more about how he's got into this situation.'
(Gay father)

'Now, he's very open is [child] and he went into school and the first year he obviously said he had two mums and he came home and he said, "They don't believe I've got two mums, they think one of you's a stepmum." So we sat down and explained that. And when I went to pick him up there were three girls there that he goes to the afterschool club with and they were like, "Does [child] really have two mums?" and I said, "Yeah," and they said, "Oh right". I don't think they've teased him for it, I think more they've tried to understand and to make sense.'
(Lesbian mother)

'We go camping quite a lot in the summer, so the kids are in and out of everybody's tent. So you'll quite often get other kids, and usually one of those kids go: "Where's [child]'s mum?" "Well, he doesn't actually have one here." "Why not?" "Well, she's not around. He's got two dads." And you can see these kind of kids going, "What? I'm sorry, I don't get that." And then, you know, sometimes they'll want to know more, because kids are great in that respect. They just come out and tell you as it is, so you just answer them. You know, in honesty. That's always been our thing – honesty – and it's served us well so far. I think if you're honest and upfront, people can't really argue with you. Or they find it very hard to argue with you.'
(Gay father)

Children at school were reported to be largely accepting.

'The kids at their primary school just accept that [child] has two mums. I'm sure it might change when they get to secondary school, but at the moment it's like, oh well, they've got two mummies – that's how it is.'
(Lesbian mother)

'Quite a few children at school ... [child]'s best friend said to her mummy, oh I don't know, at Christmas time I think, "Can I have two mummies as well? I still like Daddy, but I'd really like to have two mummies as well." And when we go to pick up, all the children will say, "Hello Mummy (Parent B)," or, "Hello Mummy (Parent A)," and if we go together, actually, if we go together, thinking about it, [child] will often jump up and down at kindergarten and say, "Look, I've got two mummies!"'
(Lesbian mother)

Many parents acknowledged that the responses of peers would be likely to change as their children grew older.

'We're under no illusions that when the kids get older or go to secondary school and hormones go a little bit crazy, kids say things and do things that they don't necessarily mean. We're under no illusions that comments will be made or things will be said ... But hopefully, by that time, our kids will have been around long enough to know how to react, and have a support network there for them.'
(Lesbian mother)

'I appreciate things may change when they get older, but there's another lesbian couple at the school, so they're not the only one.'
(Lesbian mother)

Lesbian and gay parents had conversations with their children about different kinds of families, to instil confidence in their children about their identity and help protect them from peer problems.

'We want to give them the tools to deal with questions themselves [...] we want to be able to give them the ability to say what they want to say, or just field the questions depending on who it is – whether it's a friend or someone just being nosy.'
(Lesbian mother)

'Among his circle of friends there is no issue, but you know, we are also conscious of the fact that not everybody in the wider world sees the world exactly in the same way. So I think part of it is making him feel comfortable with it so that if somebody ever threw it back at him in a mean way, hopefully it would be like water off a duck's back and he would say, "Yeah, I'm aware of that, what else have you got to say to me?", you know, that sort of attitude. So giving him a little bit of resilience around both the adoption process and having two dads.'
(Gay father)

'I think we initiated it because we didn't want them to, you know, be naive or be bullied or anything else about it. If they're up front about it and they fully understand it, then you can't be bullied, can you, or teased or whatever, if you're aware ... '
(Gay father)

'We'll talk about the differences in people [...] just whether it's the sexuality or the way they look or their weight or their colour. We're trying to make her as diverse as possible and to understand the differences and not be judgemental.'

(Lesbian mother)

Although same-sex parents recognised their children might face additional challenges, they felt that their children were effectively equipped to deal with comments made about their family. They also felt that their children would have the advantage of growing up to be tolerant of differences in others.

12 Parents' experiences of the adoption process

All parents were asked about their experiences of and during the adoption process.

When reflecting on how the agency staff and other professionals had responded to them during the adoption process, experiences were mixed; 54 per cent of gay fathers and 75 per cent of lesbian mothers felt they had experienced some negativity directed towards them during the adoption process, in comparison with 30 per cent of the heterosexual parents.

Some same-sex parents felt they received nothing but positivity from the agency and professional staff whom they encountered on their journey to adoption.

'I think the social worker and the support worker were fantastic. And there was no issue, you know, we were like any other parents that were going forward to adopt a child. Our sexuality didn't come into it. And I didn't get any sense from the panel about that either.'
(Lesbian mother)

Others received different responses from different agencies.

'Once we met [agency], it was like a breath of fresh air. They were just delighted to get their hands on us, and were nothing but empowering and respectful. They just seemed to have total and utter faith in us.'
(Lesbian mother)

A minority of families felt they received an explicitly negative response from agency staff members. For example, one gay father described having the phone slammed down on him when making initial enquiries. The staff member asked him what his wife's name was, to which he answered, 'Matt'.

'[Adoption agency member said] "Y'what? Nat?" I'm like, "No, not Nat, Matt." I mean, I ended up literally spelling it out, "M-A-T-T," and I went, "It's a bloke," and beep, the phone went down.'
(Gay father)

A lesbian mother described their experience with their first social worker.

'We had a bit of a tricky experience at first because we had a social worker who said to us, "I've come to assess you because nobody else wanted you because you were gay." '
(Lesbian mother)

For many other parents, although they did not experience explicit prejudice or negativity, homophobia may have been latent "behind the scenes". For example, some found that they were the last to be matched out of the other adopters with whom they started training, despite meeting matching criteria or not having experienced objections to a match or approval from professionals with whom they had no direct contact.

'But you know, all the people who work with us, CAMHS, the school, everybody seemed to think, you know, that we were exceptional parents. The children were doing exceptionally well, and that … and that was a credit to the way we were parenting them, and it was as though, it was all taken to panel, saying, "Oh look, this is the perfect match," and somebody's gone, "Well, that sounds a bit too good to be true, that." Do you know what I mean? I don't know. The only thing we can come to at the end of the day, is that it must be something to do with the fact that we're two women.'
(Lesbian mother)

Many couples were among the first lesbian women and gay men to approach their local authorities or adoption agencies. This may in part account for why lesbian mothers felt they experienced more problems than gay fathers, because more female same-sex couples completed the process during the first two years following the implementation of the Adoption and Children Act 2002 (which came into effect on 30 December 2005 in England and Wales) and the Adoption and Children (Scotland) Act 2007 (implemented in September 2009 in Scotland). More difficult experiences may be related to the agency's inexperience, as those adopting more recently were less likely to experience homophobia.

The issues surrounding inexperienced staff were salient for parents. For some, this inexperience became apparent when staff did not use appropriate language, seemed nervous when speaking to couples, were unwilling to ask direct questions about their sexuality or seemed to make assumptions about what a lesbian or gay relationship was like.

'At our panel it was all a bit weird, because they didn't really know how to talk to us. We were the first gay couple they'd ever come across. [...] And they didn't know how to refer to us, what to call us. They really didn't know what words to use, and they weren't, I would say, entirely appropriate.'
(Gay father)

Gay and lesbian parents were aware that their sexuality may have resulted in them having different experiences of adoption in comparison with heterosexual couples.

'We were worried about that beforehand though. You know, you hear all these horror stories of people sort of saying that you get placed with the most difficult children because you're a gay couple and things like that.'
(Lesbian mother)

Or, alternatively, that the agency staff they were working with may have been too nervous to discuss issues pertaining to their sexuality.

'We would often say, you know, you should tell us if we shouldn't do this – honesty. Not follow some idea of political correctness, and they should tell us if it's not a good idea, and then we'll stop doing it.'
(Gay father)

However, parents had particular strategies to address the problems they anticipated, in particular, by selecting agencies that they felt would work with them best. While parents in all three family types mentioned trying different agencies to get a sense of where they were most comfortable, same-sex couples researched agencies in relation to their sexuality.

'So we went to [local authority agency] because we knew that they had a positive approach – you know – some gay people had adopted.'
(Lesbian mother)

Some adopters felt that choosing the right agency resulted in better experiences of the adoption process.

'It was very positive, despite what we read or what you can read about adoption. But I would also say we're quite ... we were quite forensic in our search for the type of agency we'd go for. We went to one talk about an adoption agency and we thought, not right for us ... and we looked at the Ofsted reports, we went into a lot of detail. And again, it's a bit similar to disciplining the boys – you're sort of putting all these things to try and avert having to have a behaviour management crisis, the same with the problems with adoption, we actually did our research first.'
(Gay father)

It is interesting to note that 30 per cent of the heterosexual couples also felt that they were not treated openly and positively by the staff members and professionals they met during the adoption process. A minority of gay fathers (10%)

and lesbian mothers (15%) reported negativity for reasons other than their sexuality. These included feelings that they faced prejudice because of their class, educational status, ethnicity or gender.

> 'We got the feeling that we were perhaps too white and too middle class, overly educated.'
> (Heterosexual father)

> 'Well, we did our adoption in London and it was all quite negative in London if you're of a sort of background and race that my partner and myself are, you know, there aren't white children and all this sort of thing. And you know, in a way you experience racism towards you because you're white, to be quite honest.'
> (Heterosexual father)

> 'I think that they thought we were a bit strange because we very early on said that I would continue to work and that my partner would be at home, and they turned us down because of that … and I think that if it had been the other way around and I said I would be at home, they would have accepted us right away, and they didn't because I think they thought we were a bit odd.'
> (Heterosexual mother)

Some couples reported that they were turned away by agencies at first because of their fertility status – they were still able to have biological children – a point that seemed to undermine their commitment to adoption in the eyes of the agency staff.

> 'We had to do IVF, because they wouldn't let us adopt without having done it. Which I didn't want to do. It was actually horrible.'
> (Heterosexual mother)

Parents had mixed views about the adoption process and about their relationships with the social workers whom they encountered. Some felt that the process was not too bad, especially in contrast to their expectations, and felt that there were benefits from going through a long process, particularly with respect to learning about children and their needs.

> 'Well, it's funny because most people think oh, that's great, it's really good, but until you actually go through the adoption process you don't realise all the children have got some issues or problems at some level.'
> (Heterosexual father)

Others found the process long and arduous and expressed empathy with those who are put off.

> 'The process itself is extremely long-winded, very intrusive, and I understand why a lot of people don't go through with it, quite frankly. You've got to be pretty determined and I can understand why there are so few adopters around these days because it is a really hard process.'
> (Heterosexual father)

A common theme was that the narratives in the training courses strongly focused on the difficulties of adoption, and were labelled by some parents as a 'scaremongering exercise'.

> 'I always felt that it was always in many of these preparation groups that we went to, about the negative side of adoption. Probably too much, quite frankly. I feel that there is too much negativity involved and they always seemed to be putting you off, rather than encouraging you.'
> (Heterosexual father)

Other parents felt that they didn't get enough feedback during the adoption process, which heightened the stress and sense of vulnerability of their position within the adoption system.

'It was a strange process because you're putting your whole life on the line and she [the social worker] didn't give us anything back, and I think, you know, they cannot make you any false promises, but then we just didn't really get anything from her at all, to be honest.'
(Gay father)

Parents had similarly mixed opinions regarding their relationships with social workers. Parents often had a great deal of praise for particular social workers or the adoption teams they had met.

'Social workers that we met have always been very positive, you know, I don't know ... to some extent that's ... we've been lucky. I mean they've always been professional, but they've always been more supportive than just, "It's my job".'
(Gay father)

'We had one, pretty much one social worker all the time, who was just a complete star, she was brilliant.'
(Heterosexual father)

Others found the relationship with their social worker difficult. However, parents emphasised that, like so many aspects of the adoption process, this depended on the individual.

'We had a long and varied experience of social workers and some were very good, a few were very good, and seemed to be very empathetic and any issues that we had, any questions that we had, they really seemed to have been there done that, almost expecting us to have these issues and knew exactly how to talk to us, to encourage us, whatever. And then we had others who could have social work qualifications as long as your arm but they weren't the slightest bit empathetic. So it was very varied.'
(Heterosexual father)

The gay and lesbian adoptive parents reported diverse experiences with the adoption process, both positive and negative, and felt that many of the problems they encountered were not associated with the social workers or agency staff with whom they had direct contact, but those behind the scenes, particularly when they were waiting for matches or panel approval.

Parents reported that, as prospective parents in the adoption process, they often encountered unexplained objections or hesitations that led them to question whether homophobic prejudice delayed their progress.

Many parents adopted soon after the law changed, and were often the first gay or lesbian couple to go through the process in their local areas. Those who adopted earlier appeared to have experienced greater negativity based on their sexuality.

As indicated by parents of all family types, experiences of the adoption process varied enormously depending on the agencies and the particular staff members and professionals they encountered.

Where parents felt happy with their experiences, they often cited supportive social workers who provided encouragement, positive feedback and information. Praise was also given by those families who felt they continued to receive support after the adoption process ended.

13 Summary of findings

Having reviewed all the evidence from our study, we have found few differences between gay father, lesbian mother and heterosexual parent adoptive families. However, it is interesting to note the following.

Parents' well-being

The parents in all family types generally showed high levels of psychological well-being. The slightly higher levels of depression, anxiety, stress and relationship difficulties among heterosexual parents may reflect their experiences of infertility; same-sex couples were much less likely to have experienced infertility on their route to parenthood and were more likely to come to adoption as their first choice.

Children's well-being

Children in all three family types were functioning well. Heterosexual mothers reported their children as more likely to show symptoms of hyperactivity compared to children of gay fathers, but not lesbian mothers. As expected with adopted children, the rates of problems were somewhat higher than general population norms for the UK. Concerns that have been raised in the past that children with same-sex parents may struggle with their gender identity, or show less typical sex-role behaviour, were not supported in this study.

Child adjustment

It is clear that the majority of children in all family types were adjusting well at school and making friends. Heterosexual parents' children were found to misbehave slightly more often and slightly more seriously than children of gay fathers, but not lesbian mothers. Gay fathers' children were reported as more likely to have active friendships and to see friends more often. It is worth noting that gay fathers had children who were older when placed and had spent more time in care, leading to the expectation that these children may experience greater problems and find it more difficult to adjust. However, this was not found to be the case, perhaps because gay fathers, in particular, struggle against the odds to become parents and are extremely committed to parenting.

Parent–child relationships and family life

Parents and their children in all three groups had established positive relationships. A few differences were found, with Parent A gay fathers showing greater interaction with their child than both lesbian and heterosexual mothers, and heterosexual fathers showing slightly more disciplinary aggression than Parent B gay fathers. However, overall, there was a picture of similarity, rather than difference, with respect to parent–child relationships, as well as other aspects of family life, with same-sex families, although different, parenting in traditional ways.

Becoming a parent

In all three family types, having biological children was not always important to parents, and adoption was considered to be desirable as conceiving a child; however, this was more the case for same-sex couples than for heterosexual couples. Adoption is therefore not second best for many, but, on occasion, adoption services may believe it to be the case. Gay fathers, especially, and lesbian mothers, to an extent, had different paths to adoption than heterosexual parents; many had not tried to have biological children and had not experienced the emotional difficulties of infertility and the stress of fertility treatments. This may be significant when training same-sex adopters, because workshops on grieving for the biological children they never had may not be directly relevant to them.

Openness around adoption

Children in all three family types were receiving similar levels of contact with their birth families. However, children of gay fathers were less likely to have contact arrangements with their birth fathers fulfilled, compared, in particular, to heterosexual parents' children. Parents' feelings about contact with their child's birth families varied, with the majority feeling positive or neutral. Parents' feelings often depended upon their child's experiences with their birth family pre-adoption, and whether their child's birth family was maintaining the contact arrangements in place. Openness about adoption was extremely high in the majority of families, with all but four families having spoken to their children about their birth history and adoption. This is not to say that it is an easy process, but most parents felt that it was exceptionally important for their child to feel that they could ask questions and experience an open and honest atmosphere around the topic.

Children's experiences with same-sex parents

A similar high level of openness was experienced by children of gay and lesbian parents around the topic of having two parents of the same sex. It was important to same-sex parents that their children knew about different types of families and would be aware, as they grew older, of what this difference might mean for them. Some commentators have worried that children with same-sex parents might be ostracised by their peers because of who their parents are, but this was not supported by our research; only seven out of 81 parents reported that their children were teased about having same-sex parents. These parents were working to instil confidence in their children to help them deal with potential problems as they grew up, because many expected these to develop as their children entered secondary school.

Parents' experiences of the adoption process

Although many lesbian and gay parents had positive or mixed experiences with adoption professionals, a minority had negative experiences as a result of their sexuality. This seemed to result from a lack of understanding about how to communicate with the parents or, in extreme cases, individual opinions and prejudices that occurred behind the scenes and led to prolonged delays, which left parents uncertain and anxious. Negativity seemed to be greater for those adopting soon after the change in law. With increased experience of working with same-sex prospective adopters in the future, and with increased training, gay and lesbian parents entering the adoption system should not face the same explicit or implicit homophobia as did the "pioneers" of lesbian and gay adoption.

Although adoption support is an essential and significant part of adoption, it was not a specific focus of this research; however, it seemed that the support received varied between families but was not specific to certain family types. Adoption support appeared to play an important role in how families functioned and was highly sought but not always available.

Final comments

Overall, these three types of families were characterised more by similarities rather than differences and the children seemed to have very comparable experiences regardless of their parents' sexual orientation. All parents were highly committed to parenting and developing positive relationships with their children, who often had difficulties. Contrary to concerns raised about gay fathers in particular, these families were found to be functioning as well as, and in some ways slightly better than the comparison groups of lesbian mothers and heterosexual parents. The minor differences found may be due to the traumas of infertility that the majority of heterosexual couples and some lesbian mothers had experienced. These gay fathers were the first to have gone through the adoption process to create their families; therefore, they were highly motivated and dedicated to being parents – something that, in many cases, they had never thought of as an option when they first came out as gay. It is undoubtedly necessary to follow up these families as the children grow older. Bullying and teasing are much more of a problem in secondary schools than primary schools, thus only follow-up will reveal how things turn out in the future. These findings contribute to the small amount of existing research suggesting that adoptive gay and lesbian families provide highly positive parenting environments for children.

The final word comes from children in same-sex families. We asked them what they felt was the best thing about their family.

'They let me bounce on the bed.'
Henrietta, 7, child of lesbian mothers

'They tickle me sometimes.'
Asher, 4, child of lesbian mothers

'We always spend time together.'
Hayley, 6, child of gay fathers

'They always stroke my head and read stories to me.'
Aaron, 4, child of gay fathers

'They all care about me.'
Eve, 8, child of lesbian mothers

We would like to thank the following adoption agencies for their assistance with the study:

360 Diversity
Adoption UK – South Wales
Adoption UK
Adoption Matters Northwest
After Adoption
Barnardo's – North East
Barnet Borough Council
Be My Parent
Birmingham City Council
Blackburn with Darwen Borough Council
Borough of Poole
Bournemouth Borough Council
Brighton & Hove City Council
Bristol City Council
Buckinghamshire County Council
Calderdale Council
Cambridgeshire County Council
Camden Borough Council
Cardiff Council
City of Edinburgh Council
Coram – Adopt Anglia
Coram – London
Cornwall Council
Coventry City Council
Cumbria County Council
Derbyshire County Council
Doncaster Council
DFW Adoption
Dudley Metropolitan Borough Council
Durham City Council
Dundee City Council
East Lothian Council
East Sussex County Council
Enfield Council
Essex County Council
Family Futures
Fife Council
Flintshire County Council
Gay Dads – UK

Gloucestershire County Council
Hammersmith & Fulham Council
Haringey Council
Hartlepool Borough Council
Herefordshire Council
Highland LGBT Forum
Hull City Council
Leeds City Council
LBGT Centre for Health and Wellbeing
Liverpool City Council
London Borough of Hackney
London Borough of Hillingdon
London Borough of Richmond upon Thames
Medway Council
Merton Council
Milton Keynes Council
New Family Social
Newport City Council
Norfolk County Council
Northumberland County Council
North Tyneside Council
North Yorkshire County Council
Northamptonshire County Council
Oldham Council
PACT (Parents and Children Together)
Pembrokeshire County Council
Peterborough City Council
Pink Parenting
Portsmouth City Council
Post Adoption Centre
Proud 2 B Parents
Reading Borough Council
Royal Borough of Greenwich
Salford City Council
Scottish Adoption
Sheffield City Council

Shropshire Council
Slough Borough Council
South Tyneside Council
Southend-on-Sea Borough Council
Southwark Council
SSAFA Forces Help
Staffordshire County Council
Stoke-on-Trent City Council
Stonewall
Suffolk County Council
Swansea Council
Swindon Borough Council
Thurrock Council
Tower Hamlets Council
Trafford Council
Wakefield Council
Walsall Council
Wandsworth Council
Wigan Council
Wokingham Borough Council
Wolverhampton City Council
Worcestershire County Council
Yorkshire Adoption Agency Ltd